Title Page

Healing Through Grief:

Surviving he Loss Of A Loving Parent

The Book

Healing Through Grief: Surviving The Loss Of A Loving Parent - The Book, Volume 1

By: Angelo Quentin

Published By: FamilyLyfe Book Club, 2024

(C) Copyright, Disclaimer, & Credit Page

Published: 2024

ANGELO QUENTIN

8. Limitations and exclusions of liability: caveats to limits of liability; interpretation of limits of liability; no liability for force majeure; no liability for business losses; no liability for loss of data or software; no liability for consequential loss; aggregate liability cap under document. 9. 9. Trade-marks: trademark ownership; third-party trademarks in books, or eBooks are prohibited of use. Law and district: governing law; jurisdiction.

10. This work may not be copied, sold, or used as content in any other manner, or your name put on it until you buy sufficient legal rights to sell or distribute it as your own from us as an authorized reseller, or is tributor.

11. Every effort has been made to be accurate in this publication. The publisher does not assume any responsibility for error, or omission in its or. contrary interpretations. We do our best to provide the best information on the subject, but just reading it does not guarantee success on the subject, you will need to apply every step of the process in order to get the results you were looking for.

12. This publication is not intended for use as a source of any legal, medical, or accounting advice. The information contained in this guy may be subject to laws in the United States, and other jurisdictions.

13. We suggest carefully reading the necessary terms of the services/products used before applying, any activity which is, or, related. We do not assume any responsibility for what you choose to do with this information. Use your own and best judgment.

14. Any perceived slight of specific people or organization, and any resemblance to characters, living, dead, or otherwise real, or fiction is purely unintentional.

15. Some examples of past results are used in this publication, they are intended to be for example purposes only and do not guarantee you will get the same results. Your results may be different from ours or others. Your results from the use of this information will depend on you, your skills, your efforts, and other different unpredictable factors.

HEALING THROUGH GRIEF: SURVIVING THE LOSS OF A LOVING PARENT - THE BOOK

AdSense:

It is important for you to clearly understand that all marketing activities carry the responsibility of loss of investment for testing purposes. Use this information wise at your own risk.

Published By:

FamilyLyfe Book Club, 2024 This book is a work of fiction or non- fiction. The names, characters, and events in this book are the products of the author's imagination or are used fictitiously. Any similarities to real people, places, or events are entirely coincidental.

TITLE:

"Healing Through Grief: Surviving The Loss Of A Loving Parent" Second edition (The Book), April 2024. Copyright © 2024 Angelo Q. Kirby All rights reserved. Neither this book nor any parts within it may be sold or reproduced in any form without permission.

Copyright Notice:

© Copyright 2024 "Healing Through Grief: Surviving The Loss Of A Loving Parent" All Rights Reserved Domestic And International; intellectual property rights reserved. All rights reserved. Neither this book nor any parts within it may be sold or reproduced in any form without legal permission.

Credit To:

Canva Pro / Book Format
Hotpot.ai / Paid Images

Introduction

Losing my mother was undoubtedly the most difficult and painful experience I
have ever faced in my life. The grief I felt was overwhelming and struggled to
find a way to navigate through the depths of sorrow and loss that consumed me. It was
during this time of immense despair and heartache that I turned to writing as a means
of processing my emotions and finding solace in the darkness.

As I poured my heart out onto the pages of my journal, and book I began to realize
the transformative power of putting my thoughts and feelings into words. Writing
became a cathartic outlet for me, allowing me to express the myriads of emotions that
I was grappling with and giving me a sense of release and relief from the weight of my
grief.

Through this process of self-reflection and introspection, I gradually started to
piece together a roadmap for my healing journey. I set goals for myself that centered
around self-care, self- compassion, and self-discovery. I knew that to truly heal from
the loss of my mother, I needed to not only acknowledge and process my grief but
also actively work towards finding peace and acceptance within myself.

It was this personal journey of healing that inspired me to create my book,
"Healing Through Grief: Surviving The Loss Of A Loving Parent". I wanted to share
my own experiences and insights with others who may be struggling with the
devastating loss of a parent, in the hopes that my words could offer comfort, support,
and guidance during their grief journey.

In my book, I explore the various stages of grief that one may experience after
losing a parent, from the initial shock and disbelief to the eventual acceptance and
healing that can come with time. I delve into the importance of self-care and self-
com- passion, encouraging readers to prioritize their emotional well-being as they
navigate through the pain of loss.

I also discuss the significance of setting goals for healing, whether it be through engaging in therapy, joining a support group, or simply taking small steps toward self- improvement and growth. I believe that by establishing these goals and actively working towards them, individuals can gradually find their way toward a place of healing, acceptance, and peace.

Through my writing, I aim to offer a message of hope and resilience to those who may be struggling with the profound loss of a parent. I want to remind them that they are not alone in their grief and that by acknowledging their pain, seeking support, and setting intentions for healing, they can slowly but surely find their way towards a place of light and healing.

In sharing my personal journey and insights in "Healing Through Grief ", I hope that others will find solace, comfort, and inspiration in knowing that healing is possible, even in the face of unimaginable loss. May my words serve as a beacon of light for those who are navigating their path through grief, guiding them towards a place of peace, healing, and self-love.

Chapter 1: Understanding Grief and Loss

The Saddest Day In My Life

I stood by my mother's bedside, a silent witness to the final moments of her life. The room was hushed, filled only with the soft hum of machines and the occasional rustle of a nurse's footsteps. Outside, the world continued as normal, oblivious to the tragedy unfolding within the sterile walls of the hospital room. But for me, her brothers, sisters, daughters, nieces, nephews, granddaughters, and great-grandchildren time stood still as her family, and as I watched, the woman who had brought me into this world slip away.

Her breathing was shallow, labored, as though inhaling required her to summon all the strength she had left. I could see the lines of pain etched into her face; the frailty of her once vibrant body now reduced to a mere shell. My heart ached at the sight, knowing that this was the moment I had been dreading for so long, the moment when I would have to say goodbye to the one person who had loved me unconditionally. Tears swelled up in my eyes as I reached out to grasp her hand, the once strong grip now frail and barely there. I whispered words of comfort, of love, knowing that she could no longer hear me, but I needed to say them, nonetheless. Memories flooded my mind, a tumultuous tor- rent of laughter and tears, of joy and sorrow, all blending into a bittersweet tapestry of a life well lived

As the moments ticked by, each one stretching into eternity, I felt a deep sense of sorrow wash over me. It was a sorrow so profound, so all- encompassing, that it threatened to swallow me whole. I felt as though I was being pulled under by a tidal wave of emotions, unable to find solid ground to cling to, unable to escape the overwhelming weight of my grief.

And yet, amidst the despair, a tiny spark of hope flickered within me. It was a fragile thing, easily extinguished by the darkness of loss, but it persisted, nonetheless. It whispered to me of the resilience of the human spirit, of the capacity to endure even the most heartbreaking of tragedies. It reminded me that while my mother may be leaving this world, her love would always remain, a beacon of light shining through the darkness.

HEALING THROUGH GRIEF:
SURVIVING THE LOSS OF A LOVING PARENT

As I watched her take her final breaths, as I felt the moment of her passing wash over me like a wave crashing against the shore, I knew that I would carry her with me always. Her memory would live on in my heart, a constant reminder of the depth of love and loss that we had shared. And though the pain of her absence would never truly go away, I would find solace in the knowledge that she was at peace, free from the suffering that had plagued her in her final days.

As the room grew still and the machines were silenced, I bowed my head in silent prayer, grateful for the gift of her presence in my life, even as I mourned her absence. And in that moment of quiet reflection, I felt a glimmer of hope begin to grow within me, a seed of resilience that would carry me through the coming darkest days of grief and loss. For a while, the sadness of her passing would always be a part of me, so too would the love that had bound us together, unbreakable and eternal. And in that love, I found the strength to face tomorrow, to keep her memory alive in my heart, and to live on in her honor.

Losing a parent is one of the most devastating and life-altering experiences a person can go through. The impact of losing a parent can be profound and long-lasting, affecting every aspect of your life. In this subchapter, we will explore the numerous ways in which losing a parent can impact your life.

One of the most immediate impacts of losing a parent is the overwhelming sense of grief and loss that accompanies their passing. This grief can be all- consuming, making it difficult to focus on anything else. It is important to allow yourself to feel and process this grief, as it is a natural and necessary part of the healing process.

The Impact of Losing a Parent

ONE OF THE MOST IMMEDIATE impacts of losing a parent is the overwhelming sense of grief and loss that accompanies their passing. This grief can be all-consuming, making it difficult to focus on any- thing else. It is important to allow yourself to feel and process this grief, as it is a natural and necessary part of the healing process.

In addition to the emotional impact of losing a parent, there can al- so be practical implications to consider. For example, you may suddenly find yourself responsible for making important decisions that your parent once managed, such as managing their estate or caring for younger siblings. This added responsibility can be overwhelming, but it is important to remember that you are not alone and that there are resources available to help you navigate these challenges.

The loss of a parent can also have a significant impact on your relationships with others. You may find that you are more distant from friends and family members who do not understand what you are going through, or you may feel isolated and alone in your grief. It is important to reach out for support during this tough time, whether that means talking to a therapist, joining a support group, or simply confiding in a trusted friend.

The impact of losing a parent is unique to each individual and can vary depending on a number of factors, including your relation- ship with your parent, the circumstances of their death, and your own coping mechanisms. However, by acknowledging and addressing the ways in which losing a parent has impacted your life, you can begin to heal and move forward in a healthy and constructive way. Remember, you are not alone in your grief, and there is help and support available to help you navigate this difficult journey.

The Stages of Grief

The stages of grief that follow such a loss can be overwhelming and confusing. Understanding these stages can help individuals navigate the difficult journey of mourning the death of a loving parent. The first stage of grief is denial. It is common for individuals to initially refuse to accept the reality of their parent's death. This can mani- fest as disbelief, confusion, or a feeling of numbness. However, it is important to eventually confront the truth and begin the healing process. The second stage of grief is anger. This stage may involve feelings of frustration, resentment, or even rage towards the deceased parent, one- self, or others. It is normal to experience anger as a part of the grieving process, but it is important to find healthy ways to express and cope with these emotions.

The third stage of grief is bargaining. During this stage, individuals may try to negotiate with a higher power or with themselves in an at- tempt to bring their parent back. This can involve making promises, seeking answers, or engaging in rituals to cope with the loss. However, it is important to recognize that bargaining is a natural part of the grieving process and to eventually move toward acceptance.

The fourth stage of grief is depression. This stage is characterized by feelings of sadness, loneliness, and despair. It is common for individuals to experience a sense of emptiness and longing for their parent. It is important to seek support from loved ones, therapists, or support groups during this stage to help navigate the intense emotions that come with grieving a parent's death.

Common Reactions To Grief

The final stage of grief is acceptance. This stage involves coming to terms with the reality of the parent's death and finding a sense of peace and closure. Acceptance does not mean forgetting or moving on from the loss, but rather finding a way to honor the memory of the parent while continuing to live a fulfilling life. By understanding and embracing the stages of grief, individuals can find healing and hope in the midst of their pain.

It is important to recognize that everyone grieves in their own way. There are, however, some common reactions to grief that many people experience when they lose a parent.

One of the most common reactions to grief is denial. It can be difficult to accept the reality of a parent's death, and many people find themselves in a state of disbelief for a period of time after the loss. This is a normal reaction, and it is important to allow yourself to feel and process these emotions in your own time.

Another common reaction to grief is anger. Losing a parent can mention feelings of anger and resentment, both towards the person who has passed and towards others who may have been involved in their care. It is important to acknowledge these feelings and find healthy ways to express and release them, whether through therapy, journaling, or talking to a trusted friend or family member.

Guilt is another common reaction to grief. Many people find themselves questioning whether they could have done more for their parent, or feeling guilty for things left unsaid or undone. It is important to re- member that these feelings are normal and to try to forgive yourself for any perceived shortcomings or regrets.

Sadness and depression are also common reactions to grief. It is natural to feel overwhelmed by sadness after losing a parent, and it is important to allow yourself to grieve and process these emotions in your own time. If you find yourself struggling with feelings of depression, it is important to reach out for help and support from a therapist or counselor.

Finally, acceptance is a common reaction to grief. Over time, many people find themselves coming to terms with the loss of a parent and beginning to build a new life without them. It is important to remember that everyone's grieving process is unique, and there is no right or wrong way to grieve.

By acknowledging and processing your emotions, and seeking support when needed, you can begin to heal and move forward after the loss of a loving parent.

My Personal Loss And The Start Of My Journey

As I stood by my mother's bedside, watching her take her final breaths, my heart shattered into a million pieces. The pain of losing her was a physical thing that consumed me, leaving me feeling as though I was drowning in a sea of grief in that moment, I felt utterly alone, adrift in a world that suddenly felt cold and unfathomable.

I had always believed in a higher power, in a presence that guided and protected us through life's trials and tribulations. But as I sat there, holding my mother's cold hand, I found myself questioning everything I thought I knew. could a loving God allow such unbearable pain and loss to exist?

How could He stand by and watch as my world crumbled around me?

In the days that followed, I found myself consumed by anger and bitterness, my heart hardened by the weight of my grief. I lashed out at those around me, pushing away the love and support that was offered to me in my darkest hour. I shut myself off from the world, retreating into a shell of my own making, convinced that I was alone in my suffering.

But slowly, ever so slowly, a glimmer of hope began to break through the darkness. In my moments of deepest despair, I felt a presence beside me, a warmth that wrapped around me like a comforting embrace. I heard a whisper in the wind, a voice that spoke to me in the silence of my grief.

HEALING THROUGH GRIEF:
SURVIVING THE LOSS OF A LOVING PARENT

As I began to open myself up to this presence, to this voice, I felt a shift within me. The anger and bitterness that had consumed me began to melt away, replaced by a sense of peace and acceptance. I began to see that my mother's passing was not the end, but a new beginning, a journey that she had embarked upon long before I even knew she was gone.

In the depths of my grief, I found a new sense of purpose, a new understanding of the world around me. I saw beauty in the smallest moments, the joy in the simplest pleasures. I felt a connection to something greater than myself, a sense of be- longing that transcended time and space.

As I walked along this new path, I realized that my mother's passing had not been in vain. It had been a catalyst for my spiritual awakening, a journey that would lead me to a deeper understanding of myself and the world around me. In losing her, I had found a new sense of purpose, a new clarity that would guide me through the darkness and into the light.

So, as I stand here today, with tears in my eyes and a heart full of hope, I know that my mother's spirit lives on in me. She is the guiding light that leads me through the darkest of days, the beacon of hope that shines bright in the face of despair.

As I continue on this journey of grief and healing, I know that she is with me every step of the way, guiding me towards a brighter tomorrow.

Chapter 2: Coping Mechanisms for Grieving

It's Just so Difficult

As I sit here, trying to make sense of it all, I can't help but feel the weight of the world on my shoulders. Losing my mother has been the hardest thing I've had to face. The bond between a mother and son is unlike any other, and her absence in my life leaves a void that seems impossible to fill.

I find myself grappling with a myriad of emotions on a daily basis. From overwhelming sadness to deep-seated anger, the waves of grief come crashing down on me when I'm not expecting it. It is a roller- coaster of emotions that leaves me feeling drained and lost.

There are moments when I catch myself reaching for the phone to call her, only to remember that she is no longer there. The pain of her absence is a constant ache in my heart, a reminder of all the moments we will never get to share again. It is a reality that I struggle to come to terms with, a reality that feels so unjust and unfair.

In all this pain, I have found solace in the memories of my mother. The moments we shared, the lessons she imparted, and the love she showered on me they all serve as a beacon of light in the darkness of my grief. I hold on to these memories dearly, drawing strength from them when the pain becomes too much to bear.

I have also found comfort in leaning on my support system. Whether it is friends, or family, just having someone to talk to and lean on has been invaluable in navigating through this tumultuous time.

Opening up about my feelings, no matter how raw and vulnerable they may be, has been a cathartic process that allows me to heal and grieve in a healthy way.

I've come to realize that grief is a messy and complex process. It is okay to feel a whirlwind of emotions, to cry, to scream, to laugh in the midst of it all. There is no right or wrong way to grieve, and it is important to give ourselves the grace and space to navigate through it in our own time and pace.

So to anyone out there who is grappling with the loss of a parent, know that you're not alone. Your pain is valid, your feelings are valid, and it is okay to lean on others for support. Hold on to the memories, seek comfort in those who love you, and remember that healing is a process that takes time.

In the midst of all the pain and heartache, may you find moments of peace and solace. And may you find the strength to continue on, knowing that your parent love will always be with you, guiding you through the darkness and into the light.

In all the pain and heartache, may you find moments of peace and solace. May you find the strength to continue, knowing that your parent's love will always be with you, guiding you through the darkness and into the light.

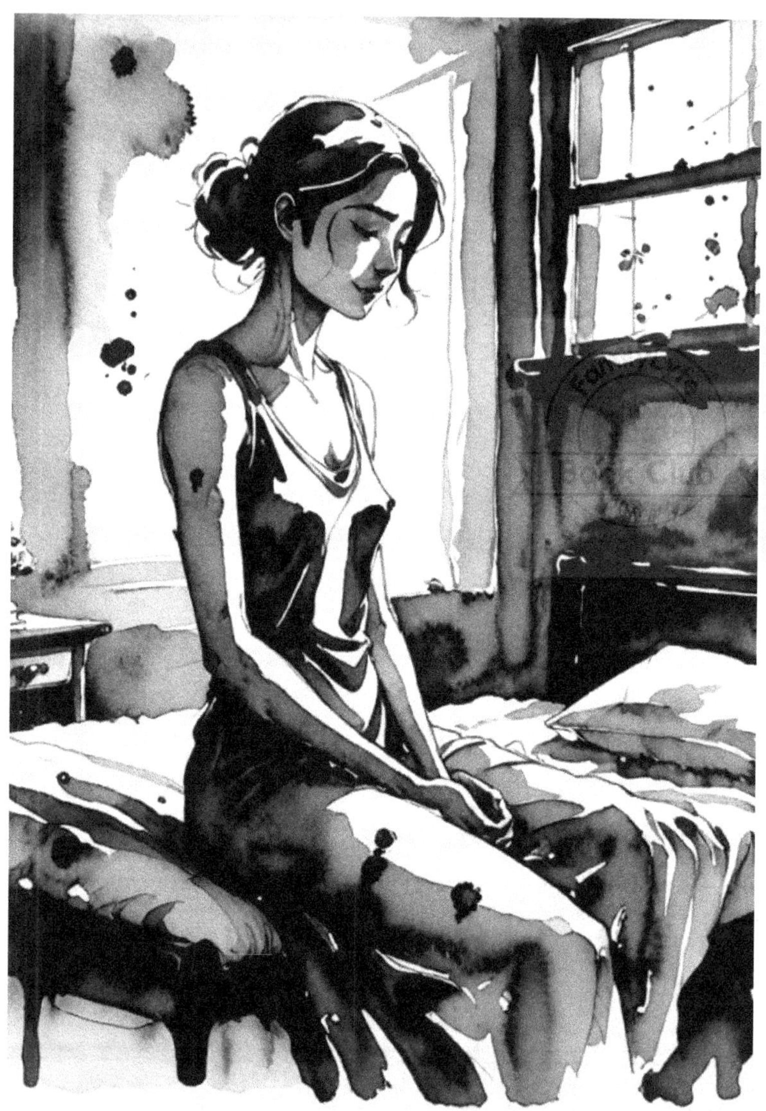

Seeking Support from Loved Ones

It is natural to feel lost and alone during grief. During this time, seeking support from loved ones can be incredibly helpful in navigating the journey of healing through grief.

Your friends and family members are there for you during this challenging time, and they can provide the emotional support and under- standing that you need.

Reach out to them and let them know how you're feeling. Share your thoughts and memories of your parent with them, and allow yourself to be vulnerable in their presence. Opening up to loved ones can help you feel less isolated in your grief and remind you that you are not alone in your pain.

Lean on your loved ones for practical support as well. They can help you with daily tasks, such as cooking meals, running errands, or taking care of your children. Allowing others to help you in this way can give you the space and time you need to focus on processing your emotions and healing from your loss.

Grief is a unique and personal experience, and everyone copes with loss in their own way. Your loved ones may not always know the right thing to say or do, but their presence and willingness to support you can make a world of difference. Be patient with yourself and with those around you as you navigate this challenging time together.

Remember that seeking support from loved ones is not a sign of weakness, but rather a testament to your strength and resilience in the face of loss. Allow yourself to be vulnerable and accept the love that others have to offer. Together, with the support of your loved ones, you can find healing and hope during your grief.

Therapy and Counseling Options

AFTER THE DEATH OF a parent, it is common to experience intense emotions such as sadness, anger, guilt, and confusion. Seeking therapy or counseling can be a crucial step in processing these emotions and navigating the grieving process. There are a variety of therapy and counseling options available to those who have lost a parent, each offering unique approaches and techniques to help individuals cope with their loss.

One option for therapy is individual counseling, where a trained therapist can provide a safe and supportive space for you to explore your feelings and work through your grief. This type of therapy can help you understand your emotions, identify coping strategies, and develop healthy ways to express your grief.

Additionally, group therapy can be beneficial for those who prefer a more communal approach to healing. Being in a group of others who have experienced similar loss can provide a sense of connection and validation, and the opportunity to share stories and support one another. Another therapy option to consider is family therapy, which involves sessions with other family members to address how the loss of a parent has affected the family dynamic.

Family therapy can help im- prove communication, resolve conflicts, and strengthen relationships within the family unit. Additionally, some may find solace in spiritual or faith-based counseling, which incorporates beliefs and practices to help individuals find comfort and meaning in their grief.

In addition to traditional therapy options, there are also alternative forms of counseling that may be beneficial for those grieving the loss of a parent. These can include art therapy, music therapy, or mindfulness practices, which offer creative and holistic approaches to healing.

These alternative therapies can help individuals express their emotions in nonverbal ways, process trauma through artistic expression, and find moments of peace and relaxation in the midst of grief.

The most important thing is to find a therapy or counseling option that feels right for you and supports your unique needs as you navigate the grieving process. Whether you choose individual counseling, group therapy, family therapy, or an alternative form of counseling, know that there are professionals ready to help you heal and move forward after the loss of a loving parent. Remember, it is okay to seek support and take care of yourself during this tough time.

Self-Care Practices for Healing

Losing a parent is a devastating experience that can leave an individual feeling lost, overwhelmed, and emotionally drained. In the chapter "Self-Care Practices for Healing the importance of prioritizing self-care during the grieving process is highlighted. In addition to the strategies discussed in the chapter, such as seeking support from loved ones and professionals, practicing mindfulness, and allowing oneself to feel all emotions, there are additional self-care techniques that individuals can incorporate into their healing journey.

One powerful self-care practice that can aid in the healing process is cultivating self-compassion. It is essential for individuals to be gentle and kind to themselves as they navigate their grief. This involves acknowledging your pain, validating your emotions, and practicing self-care activities that bring comfort and solace. Providing oneself with love and understanding can help ease the burden of grief and promote healing.

Another crucial aspect of self-care after the loss of a parent is setting boundaries. Grieving individuals may feel pressured to put on a brave face or fulfill obligations, even when they are struggling emotionally. It is important to recognize when to say no, take a break, or ask for help. Setting boundaries allows individuals to prioritize their well-being and ensure they have the space and time needed to heal.

Engaging in creative outlets is another valuable self-care strategy for coping with the loss of a parent. Whether it be writing in a journal, painting, playing music, or engaging in other forms of expression, creative activities can provide a therapeutic outlet for processing emotions and honoring the memory of the loved one who has passed away. Creating art or music may offer a sense of connection and comfort during the grieving process. My outlet for this journey was to write a book about my feelings, and then secondly I created a journal.

Engaging in creative outlets is another valuable self-care strategy for coping with the loss of a parent. Whether it be writing in a journal, painting, playing music, or engaging in other forms of expression, creative activities can provide a therapeutic outlet for processing emotions and honoring the memory of the loved one who has passed away. Creating art or music may offer a sense of connection and comfort during the grieving process. My outlet for this journey was to write a book about my feelings, and then secondly I created a journal.

Establishing a routine can also be beneficial for individuals navigating grief. While grieving can disrupt daily life and routines, creating a sense of structure and stability can provide a sense of comfort and normalcy. Setting small goals, establishing a daily routine, and incorporating self-care activities into the day can help individuals feel grounded and supported during this challenging time.

Finally, finding ways to honor and remember the loved one who has passed away can be a meaningful self-care practice. This may involve creating a memory box, planting a tree in their honor, writing letters to them, or participating in rituals or ceremonies that honor their life. Keeping the memory of the parent alive in meaningful ways can provide comfort and solace to individuals as they navigate their grief.

Incorporating these self-care practices into one's healing journey after the loss of a parent can help you navigate the complexities of grief with compassion, resilience, and grace. By prioritizing self-care, you can honor their emotions, set boundaries, engage in creative outlets, establish routines, and find ways to remember and cherish the memory of your parent. Through these practices, you can empower yourself to prioritize your well-being and emotional healing as you navigate the journey of grief.

Another self-care practice for healing is to take care of your physical health. Grief can take a toll on our bodies, leading to fatigue, poor sleep, and decreased immunity. Make sure to eat well, exercise regularly, and get plenty of rest. Taking care of your physical health can help you feel stronger and more resilient as you navigate the grieving process.

Chapter 3: Honoring Your Parent's Memory

I'll Always Remember You

I'll always remember you. Three simple words that hold so much weight, so much emotion, so much love. When we lose a parent, it can feel like our world has shattered into a million pieces. The pain is raw, the grief is overwhelming, and the emptiness in our hearts seems insurmountable. But through it all, one thing remains true - our memories of our parent will always be with us guiding us, comforting us, and reminding us of the love that will never fade.

As I sit reflecting on the memories of my mother, tears fill my eyes, and a lump in my throat. My mother was not just a parent to me, she was my rock, my guiding light, my friend. Her presence in my life was a constant source of love, warmth, and support, and her passing has left a void in my heart that can never be filled.

I remember when I was a kid the way her laughter would fill a room, her smile lighting up even the darkest of days. I remember the countless times she wiped away my tears, comforting me with her gentle words and soothing touch. I remember the way she would dance around the kitchen, singing along to her favorite songs as she cooked our family dinners.

But most of all, I remember her unwavering love for me. No matter what challenges life threw my way, my mother was always there, cheering me on, and believing in me when I didn't believe in myself. She taught me the value of kindness, compassion, and resilience, and her words of wisdom continue to guide me even in her absence.

In my own journey of grief, when I lost my mother the pain was unbearable, the tears seemed never-ending, and the void in my life felt impossible to fill. But as time passed, I realized that the memories I had of my mom were not a source of pain, but a source of comfort and strength. I found solace in reminiscing about the happy times we shared, the lessons she taught me, and the love she showered me with. I discovered that by holding onto those memories, I was keeping her spirit alive within me, a continuous light in the darkness of my grief.

I'll always remember you. These words are a promise, a vow to never forget the impact our parents had on our lives. They shaped us, nurtured us, and loved us unconditionally. And even though they may no longer be physically present, their presence is still felt in the warmth of a smile, the sound of their laughter, and the wisdom they passed down to us. Their memory lives on in the traits we inherited from them, in the values they instilled in us, and in the love that continues to flow through our veins.

It's natural to grieve, to mourn the loss of a parent who meant so much to us. But in our grief, we must also find moments of grace, of gratitude for the time we had with them, and the love they bestowed upon us. We must honor their legacy by living our lives fully, by embracing the lessons they taught us, and by spreading the love they so generously gave us. In doing so, we keep their memory alive, a flame that burns bright in the darkness of our sorrow.

I'll always remember you. These words are a reminder that our parents will always be a part of us, a guiding light in our journey through life. In moments of doubt, in times of darkness, we can turn to their memory for strength, for wisdom, and for the love that will never die. They may be gone, but their spirit lives on in us, in the way we live our lives, and in the impact we make on the world around us.

HEALING THROUGH GRIEF:
SURVIVING THE LOSS OF A LOVING PARENT

So to anyone who is struggling with the memory of a lost parent, know that you are not alone. Your grief is valid, your pain is real, but so too is the love that your parent gave you. Hold onto that love, cherish those memories, and know that you are never truly alone. Your parent's legacy lives on in you, a testament to the bond that will never break, the love that will never falter. Take comfort in knowing that their spirit is with you, guiding you, comforting you, and reminding you that you are never alone.

I'll always remember you. And in that remembrance, I find peace, solace, and love. May you too find comfort in the memories of your parent, and may their legacy continue to inspire you to live a life filled with love, compassion, and grace. Remember, you are never alone. Your parent is always with you, watching over you, guiding you, and loving you from beyond. And in that love, may you find the strength to heal, to grow, and to thrive.

As far as myself, I'll always carry my mothers memory with me every day, in the way I approach life, in the way I interact with others, in the way I strive to be the best version of myself. Her legacy lives on in the love I give to my sisters, friends, and family, in the values she instilled in me, and in the strength, she imparted through her example.

I may no longer be able to hold her hand or hear her voice, but I feel her presence all around me, in the whisper of the wind, in the warmth of the sun, in the beauty of a blooming flower. She may have left this world, but she will never leave my heart. I'll always remember you, Mom, and I will carry your love with me for the rest of my days. Thank you for being my mother, my mentor, my guardian angel. I love you, always and forever.

Creating a Tribute or Memorial

CREATING A TRIBUTE or memorial for your parent can be a healing and cathartic way to honor their memory. There are many different ways to create a tribute or memorial, and each one can be as unique as the relationship you shared with your parent.

One way to create a tribute or memorial is to gather photos and mementos that remind you of your parent. You can create a memory box filled with items that hold special meaning, such as a favorite book, a piece of jewelry, or a handwritten note. Looking through these items can bring back fond memories and provide comfort during grim times. Creating a memorial or tribute in honor of our parentis another meaningful way to keep their legacy alive. Whether it's a special ceremony, a dedicated space in our home, or even a piece of art or jewelry that reminds us of them, having a physical reminder of our parent can provide comfort and solace in times of grief. By creating lasting tribute, we can keep their memory alive for years to come.

Another way to create a tribute or memorial is to plant a tree, shrub, or flower in memory of your parent. This living tribute can serve as a beautiful reminder of their life and the love you shared. You can visit the tree or plant regularly, nurturing it and watching it grow as a symbol of the enduring bond you have with your parent.

Creating a memorial fund or scholarship in your parent's name is another meaningful way to honor their memory. This can be a way to give back to a cause that was important to your parent or to support a cause that you know they cared about. By helping others in your parent's name, you can keep their spirit alive and make a positive impact in the world.

Finally, creating a tribute or memorial can also involve sharing stories and memories of your parent with others. You can write a letter, create a scrapbook, or organize a memorial service where friends and family can come together to remember and celebrate the life of your parent. Sharing these memories can be a powerful way to keep your parent's memory alive and to find comfort in the love and support of others.

In conclusion, creating a tribute or memorial for your parent can be a meaningful way to honor their memory and find healing in grief. Whether you choose to gather mementos, plant a tree, create a fund, or share stories, the important thing is to find a way to keep your parent's memory alive in your heart. By creating a tribute or memorial, you can find comfort and solace as you navigate the difficult journey of grieving the loss of a loving parent.

Keeping Their Legacy Alive

THE PAIN OF LOSING a loving parent can leave us feeling lost and alone. However, one way to honor their memory and keep their legacy alive is by finding ways to remember and celebrate the life they lived. By doing so, we can find comfort and healing during our grief.

One way to keep our parent's legacy alive is by sharing stories and memories of them with others. Whether it's with family members, friends, or even strangers, talking about the impact our parents had on our lives can be a powerful way to keep their memory alive. By sharing these stories, we not only keep their spirit alive but also remind our- selves of the love and joy they brought into our lives.

Another way to honor our parent's legacy is by carrying on their values and beliefs. Whether it is through volunteering, charity work, or simply living our lives with kindness and compassion, we can keep their spirit alive by embodying the qualities they held dear. By living in a way that honors their memory, we can find solace in knowing that their legacy lives on through us.

Ultimately, keeping our parent's legacy alive is about finding ways to remember and honor the love they gave us. Whether it is through sharing stories, living by their values, or creating a memorial in their honor, we can find comfort and healing in knowing that their memory will never be forgotten. By keeping their legacy alive, we can find peace in our grief and continue to carry their love with us always.

Finding Meaning in the Loss

IN THE MIDST OF WHAT seems like darkness, it is possible to find meaning and purpose in the loss. This subchapter will explore ways in which we can find meaning in the loss of a loving parent and how to navigate the grieving process with grace and resilience.

One way to find meaning in the loss of a parent is to reflect on the lessons they taught us and the values they instilled in us. Our parents are often our first teachers, guiding us through life with love and wisdom. By honoring the lessons they imparted to us, we can keep their memory alive and find solace in the knowledge that their legacy lives on through us.

Another way to find meaning in the loss of a parent is to focus on the impact they had on our lives and the lives of others. Our parents shape us in profound ways, and their presence lingers long after they are gone. By recognizing the positive influence they had on us and the world around us, we can find comfort in knowing that their love and light continue to shine through us.

Finding meaning in the loss of a parent also involves embracing the emotions that come with grief. It is important to allow ourselves to feel the pain, sadness, anger, and confusion that accompany the loss of a loved one. By acknowledging and processing these emotions, we can begin to heal and find a sense of peace and acceptance in our grief.

ULTIMATELY, FINDING meaning in the loss of a parent is a deeply personal journey that requires time, patience, and self-reflection. It is important to be true to ourselves as we navigate the grieving process and to seek support from loved ones, therapists, or support groups if needed. By honoring our parent's memory, embracing our emotions, and finding purpose in our grief, we can begin to heal and move for- ward with strength and resilience giving meaning to their life and what they taught us.

Chapter 4: Moving Forward After Loss

Navigating Life

As the complexities of navigating life without my mother hit me, I was overcome with a flood of emotions. The ache in my heart from her absence is still raw, the void she left behind impossible to fill. But amidst the pain, there is a glimmer of hope, a light that guides me through the darkness of grief.

Losing a parent is a journey no one can truly prepare for. The waves of sadness come crashing over me when I least expect it, leaving me gasping for air. Simple tasks that once brought me joy now feel like a chore, a reminder of her absence. The familiar scent of her perfume lingers in the air, haunting me with memories of our time together.

But during grief, there are also moments of clarity. Moments where I am filled with gratitude for having had her in my life, for the love she showered upon me, for the lessons she imparted. I find solace in the memories we shared, the laughs we had, the tears we shed. Each memory is a precious gem, a reminder of the bond we shared and the love that will never fade.

Embracing life without my mother has been a journey of self-discovery and growth. It has forced me to confront my own mortality, to appreciate the fleeting moments we have on this earth. It has taught me to cherish the people in my life, and to express my love and gratitude openly and fearlessly. It has shown me the importance of living in the present, of savoring each moment as if it were my last.

In the midst of loss, I have found strength I never knew I possessed. I have discovered resilience in the face of adversity, courage in the depths of sorrow. I have learned that it is okay to grieve, to feel the pain of loss, to let the tears flow freely. And through it all, I have found a sense of peace, a glimmer of hope that carries me through the darkest of days.

So, to those who are navigating life without a parent, I offer these words of comfort: you are not alone. Your grief is valid, your pain is re- al. But within that pain lies the seed of healing, the promise of growth and transformation. Embrace your memories, cherish your loved ones, and hold onto hope with all your might. For in the depths of sorrow, there is also the promise of joy, of love, of a life well-lived. Embrace it, dear reader, and let it guide you on your journey of healing and moving forward after loss.

Setting Goals for Healing

THE GRIEF THAT CONSUMED me in the days and months following my Mother's passing seemed insurmountable. I felt lost, alone, and utterly broken and the thought of setting goals for healing seemed like an impossible task, one that I could not fathom taking on in that current state of despair.

It was during this dark period of my life that I decided to write the Book, and Journal, "Healing Through Grief ". I focused on the love of my sisters, and friends whose words were like angels sent to me by the Creator as a show of mercy, and I held on to their words because I knew my life depended on it. Their words offered guidance on how to navigate the tumultuous waters of grief and find a path toward healing. Through their wisdom, love, and support I could begin setting goals for my journey through grief.

One of the biggest challenges I faced was acknowledging my emotions and allowing myself to truly feel them. I had spent so much time trying to bury my pain and put on a brave face for the world that I had forgotten the importance of allowing myself to grieve. It was only when I permitted myself to feel the depths of my sorrow that I began to see a glimmer of light at the end of the tunnel.

Setting small, achievable goals for healing became my lifeline. Whether it was taking a walk in nature, journaling my thoughts and feelings, or reaching out to a therapist for support, each small step for- ward was a victory in itself. I learned to be gentle with myself, to give myself grace on the days when the weight of my grief felt too heavy to bear.

Through my journey, I discovered the power of vulnerability and connection. Opening up to friends and family about my struggles allowed me to lean on their support and find solace in their understanding. I no longer felt isolated in my pain but instead found a sense of community and love that helped me through the darkest of days.

HEALING THROUGH GRIEF:
SURVIVING THE LOSS OF A LOVING PARENT

As I reflect on my journey through grief, I am filled with a sense of hope and gratitude. While the pain of losing my mother will always be a part of me, I have learned to carry it with grace and resilience. I have found strength in my vulnerability, courage in my tears, and healing in my heartache.

To those who are navigating their journey through grief, I offer this piece of advice: be gentle with yourself, be patient with the process, and have faith that healing is possible. Set small, achievable goals for yourself and celebrate each victory along the way. And remember that you are not alone. Reach out for support, lean on your loved ones, and know that brighter days are ahead.

My journey through grief has been a tumultuous one, filled with difficulties, tears and laughter, heartache, and healing. But through it all, I have emerged stronger, wiser, and more compassionate than ever. Healing is a journey, not a destination, and I am grateful for every step that has led me to where I am today.

Setting goals for healing is an essential step in the grieving process after the loss of a parent. While it may be difficult to imagine a future without your loved one, setting small and achievable goals can help you navigate the grieving process and begin to heal. These goals can provide you with a sense of purpose and direction during a time of immense pain and uncertainty.

One important goal to set for yourself is to prioritize self-care. Grieving the loss of a parent can be physically and emotionally draining, so it is crucial to take care of yourself during this time. This can involve getting enough rest, eating well, and seeking support from loved ones or a therapist. By making self-care a priority, you can give yourself the strength and resilience needed to cope with the challenges of grief.

Another goal to consider is finding healthy ways to express your emotions. Grief can manifest in many different ways, from sadness and anger to guilt and confusion. Finding healthy outlets for these emotions, such as journaling, exercising, or engaging in creative activities, can help you process your feelings and begin to heal. By allowing yourself to feel and express your emotions, you can prevent them from becoming overwhelming or consuming.

Finally, setting goals for healing means being patient and gentle with yourself. Grieving the loss of a parent is a long and complex process, and it is important to give yourself the time and space needed to heal. By setting small, achievable goals and taking things one day at a time, you can gradually work through your grief and begin to find peace and acceptance.

Remember, healing is not a linear process, and it is okay to have good days and bad days as you navigate the difficulties of grief.

Embracing Life Without Your Parent

AS YOU NAVIGATE YOUR grief, try to focus on the positive memories you shared with your parent. Cherish the moments you had together and hold onto the lessons they taught you. Keeping their memory alive can provide comfort and strength as you move forward. In time, you may find that your grief begins to become endurable, and you're able to start envisioning a future without your parent. While they may no longer be physically present, their love and influence will continue to guide you in your journey through life. Embracing this new reality may not be easy, but with time, patience, and self-compassion, you can find a way to honor your parent's memory while still living a fulfilling and meaningful life.

As difficult as it may be, it's important to remember that it is possible to find a way forward and embrace life without your parent.

Remember embracing life without a parent is a journey that requires both time and patience. Here are some steps that may help you navigate this challenging process:

1, Allow Yourself to Grieve: It is important to acknowledge and process your emotions. Give yourself permission to feel whatever you are feeling, whether it is sadness, anger, or confusion. Remember, there is no right or wrong way to grieve. Grieving is a natural and necessary part of the healing process, and it is important to permit yourself to feel whatever emotions come up, whether it's sadness, anger, or even relief. Don't be afraid to lean on friends, family, or a therapist for support during this time.

2. Seek Support: Do not hesitate to lean on friends, family members, or a therapist for support. Sharing your feelings with others who understand can provide comfort and validation.

3. Celebrate Their Memory: Find meaningful ways to honor your parent's memory. This could include creating a tribute, participating in activities they enjoyed, or simply sharing stories about them with others.

4. Take Care of Yourself: Self-care is essential during this time. Make sure you are getting enough rest, eating well, and engaging in activities that bring you comfort and joy.

5. Find Meaning and Purpose: Look for ways to channel your grief into something positive. This could involve volunteering, pursuing a passion project, or connecting with others who have experienced a similar loss.

6. Adjust to the New Norm: Understand that life will be different without your parent, and it is okay to take time to adjust. Be patient with yourself as you navigate this new chapter of your life.

7. Create New Traditions: Establishing new traditions or rituals can help you feel connected to your parent while also embracing your own journey. Whether it is a yearly memorial event or a special activity you do in their honor, find ways to keep their spirit alive in your life.

8. Seek Meaning and Acceptance: While the pain of losing a parent may never fully go away, over time, you may find a sense of peace and acceptance. Allow yourself to find meaning in your experiences and focus on the love and lessons your parent imparted to you.

Remember, everyone's journey is unique, as you will hear me say over and over, and it is okay to take things at your own pace. Be gentle with yourself as you navigate this process, and know that healing is possible, even in the face of such profound loss.

Finding Joy and Peace in Grief

Grief is a universal human experience that can be incredibly difficult to navigate. The lost of a parent is a profound and life-changing event that can leave you feeling overwhelmed, numb, and disoriented. I would like to help provides a framework for finding moments of joy and peace amidst the pain and chaos of grief.

One of the key strategies outlined in the sub-chapter is the importance of self-care. Grieving individuals often neglect their own needs as they struggle come to terms with their loss. However, taking care of oneself is crucial in the healing process. This can involve engaging in activities that bring comfort and solace, such as taking a walk in nature, listening to music, or practicing mindfulness and meditation. Self-care can also include physical activities like exercise, eating well, and getting enough sleep. By prioritizing self-care, individuals can nurture themselves and cultivate the strength needed to navigate the complexities of grief.

Emotional expression is another vital component of the healing process. Suppressing emotions can lead to increased feelings of isolation and distress. It is important for individuals to allow themselves to feel and express their emotions, whether it be through journaling, talking to a trusted friend or therapist, or engaging in creative outlets such as art or music. By acknowledging and expressing their emotions, individuals can release pent-up feelings and begin to process their grief in a healthy and constructive way.

Seeking support is also crucial in the grieving process. Surrounding oneself with a supportive community of friends, family, or support groups can provide a sense of comfort and connection during a time of profound loss. Sharing one's feelings and experiences with others who are also grieving can create a sense of solidarity and understanding. Professional help, such as therapy or counseling, can also be invaluable in providing individuals with the tools and guidance needed to navigate through their grief and find healing.

I have personally experienced the transformative power of self-care, emotional expression, and seeking support in my own journey through grief. After losing my mother I found solace in taking long walks in the park, spending time with loved ones, and writing in a journal. These activities helped me process my emotions and find moments of peace amidst the pain. Sharing my feelings with friends and family has allowed me to gain perspective and clarity on my grief journey.

One method for finding bliss and harmony amidst pain is to permit yourself to feel your feelings. It is expected to feel a large number of feelings in the wake of losing a parent, including misery, out-rage, responsibility, and even snapshots of euphoria. Permit yourself to encounter these feelings without judgment or disgrace. By recognizing and overseeing your sentiments, you can start to recuperate and discover a genuine sense of harmony inside yourself.

HEALING THROUGH GRIEF:
SURVIVING THE LOSS OF A LOVING PARENT

It is important to acknowledge that grief is a complex and multifaceted process that can encompass a wide range of emotions, from sadness and anger to relief and even joy. It is okay to experience conflicting emotions and to honor the unique way in which grief manifests in each individual. By embracing the full spectrum of emotions that accompany grief, individuals can begin to heal and find a sense of balance and peace.

Honoring the memory of the lost loved one is also a key aspect of the healing journey. By keeping their memory alive through rituals, stories, and acts of remembrance, individuals can maintain a sense of connection and love for their parent. Creating a legacy or memorial in honor of the lost loved one can also provide comfort and solace in times of grief.

In conclusion, finding joy and peace in grief is a journey of self-discovery and resilience. It is a process of honoring the past while embracing the present and looking towards the future with hope and courage. By prioritizing self-care, emotional expression, and seeking support, individuals can navigate through the complexities of grief and find moments of healing and growth. Remember that you are not alone in your grief, and that there is beauty and strength to be found in the midst of pain. Trust in your own resilience and inner strength, and know that healing is possible, even in the darkest of times

Chapter 5: Navigating Family Dynamics After Loss

Communicating with Siblings and Extended Family

Losing a parent is a deeply challenging and emotionally charged experience that can have a profound impact on family dynamics. In the midst of grieving the loss of a loved one, navigating relationships with siblings and extended family members can become even more difficult. Effective communication becomes crucial in order to maintain healthy relationships, foster understanding, and navigate the difficult journey of grieving together.

Communicating with siblings and extended family members can be a crucial aspect of the grieving process after the loss of a parent. It is important to remember that everyone grieves differently, and each family member may have a unique way of coping with the loss. By opening up lines of communication with your siblings and extended family, you can provide each other with much-needed support and understanding during this grim time.

In my own experience, the loss of my mother brought a wave of emotions and changes to my family dynamic. Suddenly, the roles and responsibilities within the family shifted, and navigating these changes proved to be a daunting task. My siblings and I found ourselves grappling with feelings of grief, confusion, and frustration, all while trying to support each other through the pain of losing our parent.

One of the key challenges we faced was communicating our individual needs and emotions in a way that both respected our own grieving process and validated the experiences of others. It became apparent that each of us was coping with the loss in our own way, and that navigating these differences required patience, empathy, and a willingness to listen and understand.

One key aspect of communicating with siblings and extended family members is to be open and honest about your feelings. It can be helpful to have regular check-ins with each other to talk about how you are coping with the loss and to offer each other emotional support.

By sharing your thoughts and emotions with your loved ones, you can feel less alone in your grief and gain different perspectives on how to navigate this challenging time.

Practical tips that helped us navigate these complexities included setting aside dedicated time for family meetings or conversations, where we could openly discuss our feelings, concerns, and needs. Creating a safe space for open communication allowed us to address conflicts, misunderstandings, and tensions that inevitably arose during this difficult time.

Another important aspect of effective communication involved setting boundaries and expressing our needs and expectations clearly. This helped avoid misunderstandings and conflicts, and allowed us to support each other in a way that was both respectful and compassionate. For example, we made it a point to schedule regular check-ins with each other to ensure that we were all coping with our grief in a healthy and constructive manner.

In addition to communicating effectively with siblings, navigating relationships with extended family members after the loss of a parent can also pose its own set of challenges. Differences in coping mechanisms, communication styles, and expectations can lead to tensions, misunderstandings, arguments, and in worst case scenario fighting within the family unit.

It is important to listen to the experiences and emotions of your siblings and extended family members. Everyone may have unique memories and relationships with their parent, and by listening to their stories and perspectives, you can gain a deeper understanding of your shared loss. By actively listening and validating each other's feelings, you can create a sense of unity and support within your family.

During this time, it is important to extend empathy and understanding to extended family members, while also maintaining open lines of communication. This can help foster a sense of unity and support within the family, and create a space for healing and connection during the grieving process.

Real-life examples from my own journey include reaching out to extended family members for support, sharing memories and stories of our parent, and finding ways to honor their legacy together. These actions helped cultivate a sense of togetherness and unity within our extended family, and allowed us to navigate the complexities of grief in a supportive and loving environment.

Communicating with siblings and extended family members can also be a way to honor the memory of your parent. Sharing stories, memories, and traditions can help keep your parent's spirit alive and create a sense of connection with your family members. By coming together to celebrate your parent's life, you can find comfort and solace in each other's company and create new memories that honor their legacy.

The complexities of navigating family dynamics after the loss of a parent can be overwhelming, but effective communication is key in fostering understanding, maintaining healthy relationships, and navigating the grieving process together.
By setting boundaries, expressing needs and emotions openly, and extending empathy to both siblings and extended family members, we can strengthen family connections and support each other through the difficult journey of grieving. Remember to prioritize self-care, seek professional help if needed, and lean on each other for support during this challenging time. With love, patience, and understanding, we can emerge from this experience stronger and more connected than before.

Overall, communicating with siblings and extended family members can be a powerful way to navigate the grieving process after the loss of a parent.

By being open, honest, and supportive with each other, you can create a sense of unity and understanding within your family. Remember that grief is a personal journey, but by leaning on each other for sup- port, you can find strength and healing as you navigate this tough time together.

Handling Inheritance and Estate Issues

HANDLING INHERITANCE and estate issues can be a daunting task for anyone, especially when dealing with the loss of a loving parent. It is important to approach this aspect of grieving with care and patience, as it can often bring up a multitude of emotions and challenges.

One of the first steps in handling inheritance and estate issues is to gather all necessary documents and information related to your parent's assets and liabilities. This may include wills, trusts, bank statements, property deeds, and insurance policies.

Once you have gathered all necessary documents, it is important to seek legal advice to ensure that you are following the proper procedures and protocols. A lawyer specializing in estate planning can help guide you through the probate process and assist you in understanding your rights and responsibilities as an heir. It is crucial to oversee all legal matters with care and attention to detail, as any mistakes can lead to further complications down the line.

In addition to seeking legal advice, it can be helpful to communicate openly and honestly with other family members and beneficiaries. Discussing inheritance and estate issues with loved ones can help prevent misunderstandings and conflicts from arising in the future. It is important to approach these conversations with empathy and under- standing, as everyone grieves differently and may have different expectations or concerns regarding the inheritance process.

HEALING THROUGH GRIEF:
SURVIVING THE LOSS OF A LOVING PARENT

As you explore the intricacies of dealing with legacy and home issues, make sure to focus on taking care of oneself and daily reassurance. Lamenting the passing of a parent is a troublesome and profound inter- action, and dealing with yourself during this time is significant. Search for help from specialists to assist and explore the difficulties of taking care of legacy and domain issues.

Eventually, dealing with legacy and home issues can be a difficult part of lamenting the passing of a caring guardian, or parent. By moving toward this cycle with care, persistence, and backing, you can explore these difficulties with elegance and understanding. Make sure to focus on taking care of oneself, look for legitimate counsel, discuss transparently with friends and family, and look for everyday encouragement to help you through this troublesome time.

Supporting Each Other Through Grief

THE STAGGERING SORROW and feeling of misfortune can feel agonizing on occasion. Nonetheless, it is essential to recall that you are in good company in your distress. There are numerous ways of tracking down help and solace during this troublesome time.

One of the main ways of adapting to the departure of a parent is to rest on the help of others. Whether it's companions, relatives, or even a care group, having areas of strength for a framework setup can im- prove things significantly. Discussing your sentiments and recollections of your parent with other people who comprehend can assist you with managing your distress and sympathize with less alone in your torment. It's additionally essential to recollect that everybody laments un- expectedly. Certain individuals might need to discuss their sentiments and recollections, while others might like to process them in private. It means quite a bit to respect your cycle and allow yourself to process in the manner that feels right to you. There is no correct method for lamenting, and it is okay to feel a scope of feelings, from bitterness to outrage, to deadness.

Lastly, the way to endure the departure of a parent is to be delicate with yourself and give yourself an opportunity to lament. Recuperating from the passing of a parent can be a long and troublesome cycle, however, with the backing of others and the eagerness to respect your exceptional processing interaction, you can figure out how to explore through the torment and discover a feeling of harmony and mending on the opposite side.

Chapter 6: Taking Care Of Legal Obligations As A Family

Supporting Each Other Through Legal Matters

After the loss of a parent, it is crucial for family members to come together and support one another through legal matters that follow. This can be a challenging and emotional time, so it is important to lean on each other for emotional support and guidance. By working together, you can ensure that your parents' wishes are fulfilled and that legal obligations are met.

Navigating Legal Matters as a Family: Strengthening Bonds Through Unity and Cooperation in the Aftermath of Loss. In Chap- ter6 of "Healing Through Grief: Surviving The Loss Of A Loving Par- ent," we explore the crucial role that families play in supporting each other through the tangled web of legal matters that arise after the passing of a parent. From estate planning to probate, taxes to wills, the complexities of legal obligations can feel overwhelming during grief. How- ever, by coming together as a united front, families can tackle these challenges with grace and efficiency.

One of the most important aspects of addressing legal matters following the loss of a parent is ensuring that their wishes are conducted as smoothly as possible. This often involves careful attention to estate planning documents, such as wills and trusts, and navigating the probate process with diligence and precision. By working together as a family, each member can contribute their unique strengths and perspectives to ensure that all legal obligations are met, and the deceased parent's wishes are honored.

Open communication, collaboration, and shared responsibility are key components of successfully navigating legal matters as a family. By creating a supportive and cohesive environment, family members can divide tasks, share resources, and provide emotional support to each other during this challenging time. This not only strengthens family bonds but also helps to alleviate the burden of navigating complex legal processes alone.

Additionally, by working together as a family, individuals can avoid potential conflicts or misunderstandings that may arise from unclear or insufficient legal documentation. By encouraging open dialogue and transparency, families can ensure that everyone is on the same page and that decisions are made in the best interest of all parties involved.

As we delve into the importance of addressing legal matters as a family to honor the legacy of the deceased parent and ensure a smooth transition in the aftermath of loss. By approaching these challenges with unity, cooperation, and shared responsibility, families cannot only fulfill legal obligations but also strengthen their bonds and support each other through the healing process.

If Needed Finding a Neutral Mediator or Attorney

IF DISAGREEMENTS ARISE during the legal process, consider enlisting the help of a neutral mediator or attorney to help facilitate discussions and come to a resolution. Having a neutral third party can help keep emotions in check and ensure that everyone's voices are heard.

Losing a parent is a deeply emotional and challenging experience for any family. In addition to coping with grief and loss, there are also practical and legal matters that need to be addressed. Navigating legal obligations such as estate planning and distribution can often lead to tensions and conflicts among family members, making an already tough time even more stressful.

One way to ease tensions and resolve conflicts in a fair and equitable manner is to seek the assistance of a neutral mediator or attorney. These professionals are trained to facilitate discussions, mediate disputes, and ensure that all parties are heard and respected. Their impartiality and professionalism can help guide families through the complicated legal process and prevent disagreements from escalating into full-blown conflicts.

When choosing a neutral mediator or attorney, it is important to look for someone who is experienced in family law and has a reputation for fairness and ethical behavior. It is also crucial to ensure that the media- tor or attorney does not have any personal or professional connections to any of the parties involved in the dispute, as this could compromise their neutrality.

One practical way to find a neutral mediator or attorney is to ask for recommendations from trusted friends, family members, or legal professionals. It is also helpful to research online and read reviews from previous clients to get a sense of the mediator or attorney's history and approach.

Once you have a shortlist of potential candidates, it is important to schedule initial consultations to discuss your case and assess whether the mediator or attorney is the right fit for your family's needs.

During the mediation or legal process, the neutral mediator or attorney will collaborate with all parties involved to ensure that each person's interests and concerns are addressed. They will function as a neutral third party, guiding discussions, clarifying legal issues, and helping everyone reach mutually beneficial resolutions.

By providing a safe and structured environment for communication, the mediator or attorney can help prevent misunderstandings and ensure that decisions are made in a fair and transparent manner.

The goal of seeking out a neutral mediator or attorney is to facilitate open and constructive communication among family members, prevent conflicts from escalating, and guide the family towards reaching resolutions that honor the wishes and intentions of the deceased parent. By collaborating with a neutral professional, families can navigate the complexities of legal obligations in a fair and equitable manner, ensuring that everyone's needs are met, and conflicts are resolved in a respectful and amicable way.

Understanding Each Other's Needs and Wants

IT IS IMPORTANT TO take the time to understand each other's needs and wants during this process. Everyone grieves differently, and it is important to respect each other's emotions and perspectives. By communicating openly and honestly with one another, you can work towards finding a solution that works for everyone. It is crucial for family members to come together and communicate effectively to understand each other's needs and wants during this time.

One of the first steps in this process is to have open and honest discussions about the wishes of the deceased parent. This may involve reviewing their will, discussing any specific requests they made, and determining how their assets should be distributed. It is important for family members to set aside their own emotions and priorities to honor the wishes of their parent.

While navigating these legal obligations, it is also important for family members to consider each other's emotions, priorities, and de- sires. Every individual grieves in their own way, and it is important to be mindful of each other's feelings during this challenging time. By practicing empathy and understanding, family members can support each other through the grieving process and work together to make decisions that honor the memory of their parent.

In order to navigate these discussions effectively, it can be helpful to seek the advice of a lawyer or financial planner. These professionals can provide guidance on the legal aspects of settling an estate and help facilitate discussions among family members. By enlisting the help of a professional, family members can ensure that the process is managed in a fair and impartial manner.

Personal anecdotes can also be helpful in guiding family members through these discussions. Sharing stories and memories of the deceased parent can help to bring family members closer together and remind them of the love and connection they shared. By focusing on the positive aspects of their parent's life, family members can find common ground and approach the legal obligations with a sense of unity and purpose.

The key to understanding each other's needs and wants during this time is communication. By openly discussing their emotions, priorities, and desires, family members can work together to navigate the legal obligations and honor the memory of their parent's. Through empathy, understanding, and open communication, family members can sup-port each other through this challenging aspect of the grieving process and emerge stronger and more united in their love for their parent's.

Coming To A Fair Arrangement

WHEN IT COMES TO DIVIDING assets or making decisions about your parent's estate, it is important to come to a fair arrangement that considers everyone is needs and wishes. By approaching these decisions with empathy and understanding, you can ensure that everyone feels heard and respected.

Coming to a fair arrangement when it comes to dividing assets and managing the estate of a deceased parent is a crucial aspect of the grieving process. While emotions may be running high during this time, it is important for family members to approach these decisions with empathy and respect for each other's needs and wishes.

One of the key factors in coming to a fair arrangement is open and honest communication. It is important for family members to express their thoughts and feelings about the estate judgment or criticism. This can help prevent misunderstandings and conflicts from arising later. Additionally, being transparent about financial matters can help ensure that everyone is on the same page and feels included in the decision- making process.

Collaboration is also essential when it comes to making decisions about asset division and estate management. Family members should work together to produce a plan that considers everyone is needs and desires. This may involve compromise on all sides, as each person may have different ideas about how the estate should be managed. By working together, family members can ensure that the final arrangement is fair to all involved.

It is important to remember that the goal of coming to a fair arrangement is not just about dividing assets, but also about honoring the legacy of the deceased parent. This can be done by making decisions that reflect the values and wishes of the parent, as well as by keeping their memory alive in the estate management process. By approaching these decisions with empathy and respect, family members can ensure that the legacy of their parent is preserved and celebrated.

In conclusion, coming to a fair arrangement when it comes to asset division and estate management is an important part of the grieving process. By approaching these decisions with empathy and respect, family members can foster a sense of unity and understanding during a challenging time. Communication, collaboration, and compromise are key in making sure that everyone is needs and wishes are considered, honoring the legacy of the deceased parent, and strengthening family bonds.

Honoring Your Parent's While Ensuring All Parties Agree

IT IS IMPORTANT TO find a balance between honoring your parent's wishes and ensuring that all parties involved agree on the final open communication, but by keeping your parent's memory and values at the forefront, you can work towards a solution that honors their legacy.

Ensuring that all parties involved agree on the final arrangements often be a challenging and complex task. It is crucial to navigate this process with compassion, compromise, and open communication to reach a solution that everyone can agree on.

One of the first steps in honoring your parent's wishes is to gather all relevant information about their preferences for their final arrangements. This may include details about their desired funeral or memorial service, burial or cremation preferences, and any specific requests they may have had. Having this information on hand can help guide discussions and decisions with family members and other involved parties.

Additionally, it is important to keep your parent's memory and values at the forefront throughout this process. By honoring their wishes, you are not only paying tribute to them but also upholding the values and beliefs they held dear. This can provide comfort, solace during a grim time, and help maintain a sense of connection with your parent.

HEALING THROUGH GRIEF:
SURVIVING THE LOSS OF A LOVING PARENT

Compromise plays a significant role in navigating disagreements and conflicts that may arise during the decision-making process. It is essential to approach these conversations with empathy and understanding, considering the perspectives and emotions of all parties involved. Finding common ground and working together towards a solution that respects your parent's wishes can help foster harmony and unity within the family.

Open communication is key to ensuring that all parties feel heard and respected throughout the decision-making process. Encouraging honest and transparent discussions can help identify potential areas of disagreement and work towards finding mutually agreeable solutions. It is essential to listen to each other's viewpoints with empathy and compassion, allowing space for everyone to express their thoughts and feelings.

Practical tips for navigating this process include creating a detailed plan outlining your parent's wishes, discussing it with all involved parties, and seeking mediation or professional guidance if needed. Remember that it is okay to seek outside support and assistance to help facilitate discussions and navigate any conflicts that may arise.

By approaching the process of honoring your parent's wishes with sensitivity and empathy, you can work towards a solution that respects their legacy while fostering unity and harmony within the family. Keeping their memory and values at the forefront can provide comfort and solace during a challenging time, allowing you to honor their legacy in a meaningful and impactful way.

Ensuring Legal Obligations are Met and Respected

FINALLY, IT IS IMPORTANT to ensure that all legal obligations are met and respected throughout the process. This includes following any legal documents or instructions left by your parent, as well as collab- orating with legal professionals to ensure that all necessary steps are taken. By staying organized and proactive, you can navigate the legal process with confidence and peace of mind.

Ensuring that legal obligations are met and respected is an important part of grieving, as it not only helps the memory of the deceased parent but also helps bring closure to the family as they navigate the challenging time of loss.

One of the first things to consider after the passing of a parent is their estate planning and will. It is essential to locate and review these documents to understand their wishes and ensure that their assets are distributed according to their wishes. If there is no will, the laws of intestacy will dictate how the estate is divided among family members. This can sometimes lead to disputes and further complications, so it is crucial to have open and honest communication with all family members to address any concerns or disagreements.

Inheritance is another important legal matter that needs to be addressed after the loss of a parent. It is important to understand the process of probate, where the court validates the will and ensures that assets are distributed correctly.

It is essential to collaborate with a qualified attorney who specializes in probate to navigate this process smoothly and efficiently. They can provide guidance on legal matters, such as tax implications and asset distribution, to ensure that all legal obligations are met.

Approaching these sensitive topics with care and respect is crucial when dealing with family members who are grieving the loss of a loved one. It is important to have open and honest communication and to listen to the wishes of the deceased parent to ensure that their legacy is honored and respected. This can sometimes lead to difficult conversations, but addressing these matters head-on can prevent future conflicts and ensure that everyone's needs are met.

When my mother passed away, we had to navigate the intricate process of her belongings. It was a challenging time for our family, but we found solace in knowing that we were fulfilling her wishes and ensuring that her legacy was honored. Working together and supporting each other during this challenging time helped us come together as a family and find strength in each other.

In conclusion, ensuring that legal obligations are met and respected after the loss of a parent is an important part of the grieving process. By approaching these matters with care and respect, families can honor the memory of their loved one and navigate the legal process with understanding. It is essential to seek the guidance of qualified professionals and work together as a family to address these sensitive topics, ensuring that all legal responsibilities are fulfilled in a way that honors the memory of the deceased parent.

Chapter 7: Remembering Your Parent's Love

She Always Showed Me Love

In the depths of grief and loss, I find comfort in the memories of my beloved mother, who always showed me love in the most profound ways. My heart aches with the knowledge that she is no longer physically present in my life, but her love continues to envelop me like a warm embrace, comforting me in my sorrow.

From my earliest childhood memories, my mother's love was a constant and unwavering presence in my life. She had a way of making even the most mundane moments special with a gentle touch, a kind word, or a knowing glance that communicated her love for me in ways that words could never fully express. Whether she was tucking me into bed at night, preparing my favorite meals, or simply sitting with me in quiet companionship, her love was a beacon of light in my world.

One of my most cherished memories of my mother is the way she would always hold my hand when we walked together. Her touch was gentle and reassuring, grounding me in the knowledge that I was loved and cared for. In those moments, the world seemed to fade away, and all that mattered was the connection between us, a bond that transcended time and space.

HEALING THROUGH GRIEF:
SURVIVING THE LOSS OF A LOVING PARENT

My mother had a way of making me feel seen and valued, even in my most vulnerable moments. She had an uncanny ability to understand the depths of my soul, offering words of wisdom and comfort when I needed them most. Her presence was like a balm to my wounded heart, healing me with her love and understanding.

There were times when my mother's love was expressed through actions rather than words. I remember how she would always save the last bite of dessert for me, knowing that it was my favorite. Or how she would stay up late into the night, listening to me talk about my worries and fears, offering a listening ear and a shoulder to cry on. Her love was tangible and real, a force that shaped me into the person I am today.

As I navigate the difficult journey of grief and loss, I find myself turning to the lessons that my mother taught me through her love. She showed me the importance of kindness, compassion, and empathy, values that continue to guide me as I navigate the complexities of life without her by my side. Her love is a legacy that lives on in my heart, a source of strength and comfort in my darkest moments.

Though my mother may no longer be physically present in my life, her love continues to surround me like a warm and comforting blanket. In moments of sorrow and despair, I draw upon the memories of her love, finding solace in the knowledge that she will always be with me, guiding me with her gentle spirit and unwavering love.

HEALING THROUGH GRIEF:
SURVIVING THE LOSS OF A LOVING PARENT

In the quiet moments of reflection, I feel my mother's presence all around me, in the gentle breeze that rustles the leaves, in the warmth of the sun on my face, and in the loving embrace of those who hold me close. Her love is a beacon of light in the darkness, guiding me through the stormy seas of grief and loss, offering comfort and solace in the knowledge that I am never truly alone.

As I continue to navigate the difficult terrain of grief and loss, I take comfort in the knowledge that my mother's love will always be with me, a guiding light in the darkness, a source of strength and comfort in my time of need. She may be gone from this world, but her love endures, a timeless and eternal force that will never fade. In her love, I find healing, in her love, I find peace. She always showed me love, and for that, I am eternally grateful.

Cherishing Memories and Moments

DURING GRIEF AND LOSS, it can be easy to get caught up in the pain and sadness of the present moment. In any case, it means a lot to make a stride back and value the recollections and minutes that we im- parted to our caring parents. These recollections are valuable fortunes that can acquire solace and recuperate the middle of our pain.

This can be a helpful and therapeutic method for regarding their memory and keeping them near our souls. Glancing back through the thoughts can bring back affectionate recollections and assist us with feeling substantially associated with our parents.

One more method for valuing recollections and minutes is to impart stories and tales to loved ones. Discussing our parents and thinking back about the great times can be a mending experience that unites us and fortifies our bond with friends and family. These common recollections can likewise assist us with feeling less alone in our sadness and give us a feeling of solace and backing.

Taking time to reflect on the special moments we shared with our parents can also help us find peace and acceptance in our grief. Remembering the love, laughter, and joy that we experienced together can bring a sense of gratitude and appreciation for the time we had with them. These memories can serve as a source of strength and inspiration as we navigate the difficult journey of grieving the loss of a loving parent.

In the end, cherishing memories and moments is a way to honor the legacy of our parent and keep their spirit alive in our hearts. By holding onto these precious memories, we can find comfort, solace, and healing in our grief. Remembering the love and joy that we shared with our parents can bring light into the darkness of our sorrow and help us find peace and healing as we continue to navigate the journey of grief and loss.

Finding Comfort in Shared Experiences

FINDING COMFORT IN sharing experiences with others who have also lost a parent can be incredibly healing. Connecting with people who utterly understand your pain and can offer support and empathy can make a world of difference in your grief journey.

One way to find comfort in shared experiences is to seek out support groups for individuals who have lost a parent. These groups pro- vide a safe space for sharing your thoughts and feelings with others who are going through a similar journey. Hearing the stories of others and knowing that you are not alone in your grief can provide a sense of comfort and validation.

Another way to connect with others who have experienced the loss of a parent is through online forums and social media groups. These virtual communities can be a valuable source of support, as they allow you to connect with people from all over the world who are going through similar struggles. Sharing your story and listening to the experiences of others can help you feel less isolated in your grief.

Attending grief workshops or counseling sessions specifically tailored for individuals who have lost a parent can also be a beneficial way to find comfort in shared experiences. These sessions provide a structured environment for processing your emotion sand connecting with others who are on a similar healing journey. It can be reassuring to know that there are resources available to help you navigate your grief and find solace in the company of others who understand.

Ultimately, finding comfort in sharing experiences with others who have lost a parent can be a powerful tool in your healing process. By connecting with individuals who can offer support, empathy, and understanding, you can find solace in knowing that you are not alone in your grief. Sharing your story, listening to the experiences of others, and seeking out support resources can help you navigate the difficult journey of grieving the loss of a loving parent.

Keeping Their Love Alive in Your Heart

THE AGGRAVATION OF their nonappearance can feel overpowering, and it might appear to be difficult to envision existence without them.

Notwithstanding, it is essential to recollect that their adoration lives on in our souls, even after they are no more. Keeping their affection alive in your heart is a fundamental piece of the lamenting system, and can assist you with tracking down solace and recuperating amidst your misfortune.

One way to keep your parent's love alive in your heart is to cherish the memories you shared. Reflecting on the happy times you spent with them can bring a sense of peace and connection, reminding you of the love you shared. Whether it is looking through old photos, re-reading letters or emails, or simply thinking back on special moments, holding onto these memories can help you feel close to your parent even after they are no longer physically present.

One more method for keeping your parent's adoration alive in your heart is to continue their heritage. Ponder the qualities, convictions, and customs that were critical to your parent, and endeavor to respect them in your own life.

Whether it is chipping in for a purpose they often thought about, proceeding with a family custom, or carrying on with your life in a manner that would do right by them, tracking down ways of keeping their soul alive can assist you with a feeling associated with them and track down significance in your sadness.

It can also be helpful to find ways to express your love for your parent even after they have passed away. Writing letters, keeping a journal, or talking to them in your thoughts can be powerful ways to communicate your feelings and keep their memory alive, or dedicate a special day to celebrating their life.

Ultimately, keeping your parent's love alive in your heart is a deeply personal journey that will look different for everyone. It is important to permit yourself to grieve in your own way and at your own pace, knowing that it is okay to feel a mix of emotions as you navigate this tough time. By holding onto the love you shared with your parent and finding ways to honor their memory, you can find healing and comfort in your grief, knowing that their love will always be a part of you.

Chapter 8: Finding Hope and Healing

As I sat in the quiet solitude of my mother's room, surrounded by the familiar scent of her favorite perfume lingering in the air, I could not help but feel the weight of her absence pressing down on me. It had been three months since she took her last breath, leaving me to navigate the turbulent waters of grief on my own. The pain was raw and unrelenting, threatening to swallow me whole at any moment.

Even in the darkest moments of despair, I clung to a tiny glimmer of hope that flickered deep within me being stubborn and refusing to be extinguished. It was a fragile thread that connected me to my mother's memory, reminding me of her unwavering love and the strength she instilled in me throughout my life.

And it was this sliver of hope that guided me through the stormyseas of grief, leading me towards a place of healing and acceptance.

In my sorrow, I found solace in the words of Martha Whitmore Hickman, who once said, "Grief is the price we pay for love." Those simple words resonated deeply within me, serving as a poignant reminder of the profound bond I shared with my mother. The intensity of my grief was a testament to the depth of my love for her, and I knew that I would carry her memory in my heart forever.

HEALING THROUGH GRIEF:
SURVIVING THE LOSS OF A LOVING PARENT

As I began to navigate the complex emotions swirling within me, I turned to the wisdom of Marisa Renee Lee, who spoke of the importance of selfcare and compassion during times of grief. I allowed my.

As I began to navigate the complex emotions swirling within me, I turned to the wisdom of Marisa Renee Lee, who spoke of the importance of selfcare and compassion during times of grief. I allowed myself to embrace the waves of sorrow that washed over me, allowing the tears to fall freely without shame or restraint. I sought comfort in simple rituals that reminded me of my mother's presence, like brewing a pot of her favorite tea or lighting a candle in her honor. Through it all, I treated myself with kindness and patience, recognizing that healing was a gradual process that required time and tenderness.

In moments of profound sadness, I found solace in the poetry of Anne Foster, whose words spoke to the ache in my soul with haunting beauty. I allowed myself to grieve openly and honestly, acknowledging the raw pain that threatened to consume me. I sat with my sorrow and allowed it to wash over me like a cleansing rain, trusting that each tear shed was a tiny step toward healing.

As I journeyed through the labyrinth of grief, I discovered a sense of resilience that surprised even me. Despite the overwhelming sorrow that threatened to engulf me, I found the strength to continue, buoyed by the love and memories of my mother. I knew that she would want me to find peace and joy in life once more, to honor her memory by living fully and authentically.

In the quiet moments of reflection, I found a glimmer of hope that shone brightly within me like a beacon in the darkness. I knew that my mother's spirit was watching over me, guiding me toward a place of healing and wholeness. And as I embraced the pain of my loss with an open heart, I knew that I would never truly let go of hope. For in hope, I found the courage to face each new day with grace and gratitude, knowing that my mother's love would always be with me, lighting my way through the shadows of grief.

Embracing the Journey of Grief

IT IS CRITICAL TO RECALL that distress is a characteristic and vital piece of the recuperating system. Embracing the excursion of despondency implies permitting yourself to feel each of the feelings that accompany losing a parent, regardless of how troublesome or difficult they might be.

One of the most vital phases in embracing the excursion of sorrow is to permit yourself to completely feel your feelings. It is okay to feel miserable, furious, and befuddled after the demise of a parent. These feelings are every one of the typical pieces of the lamenting system, and attempting to smother them or push them away will just draw out your torment. Allow yourself to feel anything that you are feeling, and realize that it is each of the pieces of the mending system.

One more significant part of embracing the excursion of distress is to look for help from others. Grieving the departure of a parent can feel unbelievably detaching, yet it is critical to recall that you are in good company. Contact companions, relatives, or a specialist who can offer you solace, understanding, and backing during this troublesome time.

Discussing your sentiments and encounters can assist you with managing your pain and starting to mend. It is additionally essential to contemplate, and investing energy in self- awareness can be a useful way of adapting to despondency and dealing with yourself during this troublesome time.

At long last, recollect that mending from the departure of a parent is an excursion, not an objective. Distress does not have a timetable, and everybody processes their feelings in their specific manner and at their speed.

Show restraint toward yourself, and realize that it is okay to feel a great many feelings as you explore this troublesome time. Embracing the excursion of sorrow implies permitting yourself to feel, looking for help from others, dealing with yourself, and recalling that mending is a cycle that requires some investment.

Seeking Professional Help When Needed

GRIEF IS A COMPLEX and individual process, and there is no right or wrong way to grieve. However, sometimes the pain can become too much to bear on your own, and that is when it is important to reach out for help.

Specialists and instructors are prepared experts who can offer help and direction as you explore the lamenting process. They can assist you with managing your feelings, foster survival methods, and track down ways of regarding and recollecting your parent. Conversing with a specialist can likewise assist you with feeling less alone in your despondency, as they can offer a protected and nonjudgmental space for you to communicate your sentiments.

Support bunches are one more important asset for those lamenting the passing of a parent. These gatherings give a steady local area of people who are going through comparative encounters. Talking about your thoughts with other people who comprehend can be unquestionably approving and soothing. Support gatherings can likewise give down-to- earth guidance and assets to adapting to despondency, as well as any open doors to interface with other people who are further along in their melancholy process.

In some cases, medication may be necessary to help manage the symptoms of grief, such as depression or anxiety. If you are struggling to function in your day-to-day life or experiencing severe emotional dis- tress, it may be helpful to speak with a psychiatrist about medication options. While medication is not a cure for grief, it can help alleviate some of the more intense symptoms and make it easier to navigate your grief journey.

Remember, seeking professional help is not a sign of weakness, but rather a sign of strength and self-care. Grieving the loss of a parent is a deeply personal and complicated process, and it is important to prioritize your mental and emotional well-being during this challenging time.

Whether you choose to see a therapist, join a support group, or explore medication options, know that there are resources available to help you through your grief and support you on your journey toward healing.

Moving Forward With Strength and Resilience

KEEPING IN MIND OTHERS have walked this path before us, and who have found ways to navigate through pain and find healing. It is not easy to move forward with strength and resilience. It requires us to tap into our inner self-power.

Finding a balance between honoring our loved one's memory and finding a way to live our lives in a meaningful and fulfilling way is what moving forward with strength and resilience is about. We can find strength and resilience by allowing ourselves to grieve, and take care of ourselves. it is critical to be in good company in our sadness.

Pushing ahead with strength and versatility is not a simple assignment, yet it is conceivable. It expects us to take advantage of our inward place of mental fortitude and assurance, and to rest on the help of other people who care about us. It is critical to recall that sadness is an inter- action and that it requires investment to recuperate. There will be great days and terrible days, yet with persistence and determination, we can track down our direction through obscurity.

One method of pushing ahead with strength and versatility is to permit ourselves to completely feel our feelings. It is all right to feel miserable, irate, or even numb. These sentiments are a characteristic piece of the lamenting system, and it is vital to recognize them and al-low ourselves to completely encounter them. By permitting ourselves to feel our feelings, we can start to manage our pain soundly, and overall track down recuperation and harmony.

Eventually, pushing ahead with strength and versatility is tied in with finding harmony between respecting our cherished one's memory and figuring out how to continue with our lives in a significant and satisfying manner. By permitting ourselves to lament, looking for help from others, and dealing with ourselves, we can find the strength and flexibility we want to push ahead and track down recuperating after the passing of a caring parent.

Chapter 9: Resources for Grieving Children and Teens

Helping Children Understand and Process Grief

Losing a parent is one of the most difficult experiences a child can go through. As a parent facing this situation, it is important to help your child understand and healthily process their grief. By providing support and guidance, you can help them navigate through their emotions and begin to heal.

One of the first steps in helping children understand and process grief is to be open and honest with them about the situation. It is important to explain to them what death means and answer any questions they may have. Encourage them to express their feelings and emotions, whether it be sadness, anger, confusion, or fear. Let them know that it is okay to grieve and that you are there to support them through this grim time.

It is also important to create a safe and supportive environment for your child to express their grief. Encourage them to talk about their feelings, memories of their parent, and any worries or concerns they may have. Let them know that it is normal to feel a wide range of emotions and that you are there to listen and provide comfort. Encourage them to participate in activities that help them process their grief, such as journaling, drawing, or talking to a therapist.

As a parent, it is important to model healthy grieving behaviors for your child. Show them that it is okay to cry, to talk about their feelling.

Let them know that it is normal to feel a wide range of emotions and that you are there to listen and provide comfort. Encourage them to participate in activities that help them process their grief, such as journaling, drawing, or talking to a therapist.

As a parent, it is important to model healthy grieving behaviors for your child. Show them that it is okay to cry, to talk about their feelings, and to seek support from others. By demonstrating healthy coping mechanisms, you can help your child learn how to navigate their grief constructively.

Encourage them by reaching out to friends, family members, or support groups for additional help and guidance.

Finally, remind your child that healing takes time and that it is a process. Encourage them to be patient with themselves and help them to take care of their physical and emotional well-being. Let them know that it is okay to seek profession- al help if they are struggling to cope with their grief. By pro- viding your child with love, support, and guidance, you can help them understand and process their grief in a way that allows them to heal and move forward healthily.

Supporting Teenagers Through Loss

LOSING A PARENT IS an incredibly difficult experience for anyone, but for teenagers, it can be especially challenging. Adolescents are al- ready navigating the difficulties of growing up, and the loss of a parent can add an extra layer of complexity to an already tumultuous time. As parents dealing with the death of their partner, it is important to provide support and understanding to your teenager as they grieve.

One of the most important things you can do to support your teenager through the loss of a parent is to keep communication open. Encourage them to express their feelings and talk about their emotions, even if it is difficult for them. Be patient and listen without judgment, allowing them to process their grief in their way and at their own pace. It is also important to provide a sense of stability and routine for your teenager during this tough time. Try to keep their daily routine as normal as possible, even as you both navigate the changes that come with the loss of a parent. This can help provide a sense of security and predictability during a time of great uncertainty.

Encourage your teenager to seek out support from friends, family, or a therapist who specializes in grief counseling. Sometimes teenagers may be hesitant to reach out for help, but having a support system in place can make a substantial difference in their healing process. Let them know that it is okay to ask for help and that they do not have to go through this alone.

Lastly, be gentle with yourself as you support your teenager through their grief while also coping with your own. It is okay to not have all the answers or to feel overwhelmed at times.

Remember that healing takes time, and it is important to be patient and kind to your- self and your teenager as you both navigate the grieving process together. By providing love, support, and understanding, you can help your teenager through this challenging time and guide them towards healing and resilience in the face of loss.

Connecting with Grief Support Organizations and Programs

IT IS IMPORTANT TO seek out support during this challenging time. One way to connect with others who are going through similar experiences is by getting involved with grief support organizations and programs. These organizations offer a range of resources and services to help individuals navigate the grieving process and find comfort and healing in their time of need.

One of the benefits of connecting with grief support organizations is the opportunity to meet others who are also grieving the loss of a parent. Being able to share your feelings and experiences with people who understand what you are going through can be incredibly comforting and validating. Grief support groups provide a safe and supportive space for individuals to express their emotions, ask questions, and receive guidance from trained professionals and peers who have been through similar situations.

In addition to the emotional support provided by grief support organizations, many programs also offer practical resources and tools to help individuals cope with their loss. This can include information on managing grief symptoms, accessing counseling services, and learning healthy coping strategies. By participating in these programs, individuals can gain valuable insights and skills that can help them navigate the grieving process and begin to heal in a healthy and productive way.

HEALING THROUGH GRIEF:
SURVIVING THE LOSS OF A LOVING PARENT

Grief support organizations also often host workshops, seminars, and events that provide education and information on grief and loss. These events can be a valuable source of knowledge and guidance for individuals who are struggling to come to terms with their parent's death. By attending these programs, individuals can learn more about the grieving process, connect with experts in the field, and gain insights into how to cope with their loss in a healthy and constructive manner.

Overall, connecting with grief support organizations and programs can be a crucial step in the healing process for individuals who have lost a parent. By seeking out support, resources, and education through these organizations, individuals can find comfort, connection, and healing as they navigate the difficult journey of grief. Whether through support groups, workshops, or counseling services, these organizations offer a valuable lifeline for those who are struggling to cope with the profound loss of a loving parent.

Chapter 10: Conclusion

It's Been A Year Now

It's been a year now, A year since I lost the anchor of my world, the one who held me close and whispered words of love and encouragement in my ear. A year of navigating the tumultuous waters of grief, of learning to let go and hold on to memories with equal measure. In the quiet moments when the world seems to be still, the ache in my heart is still raw and unfiltered like a loud freight train going by, I find myself grappling with the enormity of this loss.

There are days when the grief feels like a heavy cloak, weighing me down and making it hard to breathe. The memories flooded back, washing over me in a tide of sorrow and longing. I miss her laughter, her comforting presence, her way of making even the darkest days seem a little brighter. How do you go on without the one who taught you how to navigate the highs and lows of life?

But in this darkness, there is a flicker of light. A glimmer of hope that reminds me that even in the depths of despair, there is a way forward. I have learned that grief is not a linear journey, but a winding path that twists and turns, leading me through valleys of sorrow and peaks of fleeting joy. And in this journey, I have discovered a resilience I never knew I possessed.

I have become intimately acquainted with the bittersweet nature of memory. How a passing scent or a familiar melody can transport me back to a moment of joy shared with my mother, only to leave me breathless with the knowledge that she is no longer here to share in those moments. But I have also learned to treasure these memories, to hold them close like precious jewels that illuminate the darkness of grief.

HEALING THROUGH GRIEF:
SURVIVING THE LOSS OF A LOVING PARENT

There have been moments of anger and frustration, moments when I have raged against the unfairness of it all. Why did she have to leave? Why was I robbed of the chance to grow older with her by my side? But in those moments, I have also found a wellspring of strength within me, a determination to honor her memory by living my life with purpose and love.

I have sought solace in the embrace of loved ones, in the shared laughter and tears that remind me I am not alone in this journey. I have found comfort in the words of strangers who have walked this path before me, who have offered me their wisdom and guidance in the darkest moments of my grief. And in their kindness, I have found a seed of hope that has begun to blossom within me.

So as I mark this one-year milestone, I do so with a heart heavy with sorrow but also light with the promise of healing. I am learning to live with the absence of my mother, to carry her memory with me like a beacon that guides me through the stormy seas of grief. And in this journey, I have discovered a depth of resilience and compassion that I never knew I possessed.

To those who are on a similar path, and who are grappling with the loss of a beloved parent, I offer this message of hope: you are not alone. Your grief is valid, your pain is real, but so too is the possibility of healing.

Embrace the memories, honor the love that once was, and know that in time, the ache in your heart will soften, and the light of hope will shine once more. It has been a year now, but the journey continues, and with each step forward, we find the strength to heal.

Andy
Evie
Marty

Reflecting on Your Grief Journey

AS YOU NAVIGATE THE difficult path of grieving the loss of a loving parent, it is important to take time to reflect on your grief journey. Reflecting on your emotions, thoughts, and experiences can help you process your feelings and find healing during your pain. It is normal to experience a wide range of emotions after the death of a parent, including sadness, anger, guilt, and even relief. Taking the time to acknowledge and understand these emotions can help you come to terms with your loss and begin to heal.

One way to reflect on your grief journey is to journal about your feelings and experiences.

Writing down your thoughts can help you make sense of your emotions and provide a record of your journey through grief. You may also find it helpful to talk to a therapist or counselor about your grief, as they can provide support and guidance as you navigate this challenging time. Sharing your feelings with trusted friends and family members can also be beneficial, as they can offer comfort and understanding as you grieve.

It is important to remember that everyone grieves differently, and there is no right or wrong way to mourn the loss of a parent. Some people may find solace in participating in rituals or traditions that honor their parent's memory, while others may prefer to find comfort in solitude. Whatever your coping mechanisms may be, it is important to permit yourself to grieve in your own way and at your own pace. Remember to be gentle with yourself and allow yourself the time and space you need to heal.

High-Lights: Finding Peace and Acceptance In the Loss of Your Parent

AS I SIT HERE, PEN in hand, trying to find the words to express the depth of emotions swirling within me, I am reminded of the journey I have been on since the passing of my mother. The pain of her absence is a constant ache in my heart, a void that seems impossible to fill. But through this storm of grief, I have found moments of peace and acceptance, small glimmers of light in the darkness.

My mother was my rock, my anchor in the stormy seas of life. Her presence was a source of comfort and strength, and her absence has left me feeling adrift, lost in a sea of sorrow and confusion. The pain of losing her is a wound that will never fully heal, a scar that will always be a part of me. But during this pain, I have found moments of profound clarity and understanding.

I have come to realize that grief is not a sign of weakness, but of love. It is a testament to the deep bond we share with our loved ones, a reflection of the depth of our emotions and the strength of our connection. Grief is a journey, a path we must walk with courage and grace, allowing ourselves to feel the pain and sorrow without being consumed by it.

In the days and weeks following my mother's passing, one of the most powerful tools in my healing journey has been the power of forgiveness. I have learned to forgive myself for the moments of anger, frustration, and sorrow that have consumed me in the wake of my mother's passing. Some of you will have to learn to forgive your parent for also leaving you too soon, and for not being there to guide you through this tumultuous time.

Most importantly, some of you are asking God why is he allowing this pain and sorrow into your life, questioning God's plan, and you're now doubting His love, or feeling as though he has abandoned you in your darkest hour, but please trust me he has not, he's the voice you're hearing telling you everything will be okay, you're not alone.

Through forgiveness, I have found a sense of peace and acceptance that I never thought possible. I have learned to let go of the anger and bitterness that threatened to consume me, and instead embrace the love and memories that my mother left behind. I have learned to see her passing not as a tragedy, but as a gift, a reminder of the preciousness of life and the beauty of love.

But perhaps the most profound lesson I have learned in the wake of my mother's passing is the power of faith. I have always considered my- self a spiritual person, but in the face of such overwhelming grief, my faith was tested in ways I never thought possible.

But through it all, I never lost sight of the fact that my mother's passing was not the end, but a new beginning. I have felt her presence in the gentle breeze that rustles the leaves, in the warmth of the sun on my face, and in the love and support of friends and family who have stood by my side through this tough time. I have come to believe that my mother is not truly gone, but merely transformed, her spirit living on in the love and memories she left behind.

In the months since my mother's passing, I have begun to find moment of peace and acceptance, small steps toward healing and hope. I know that the road ahead will not be easy and that there will be days when the pain and sorrow threaten to overwhelm me once again. But I also know that I am not alone, that my mother's love surrounds me, guiding me through the darkness toward the light.

And so I take each day as it comes, allowing myself to feel the pain and sorrow, but also embracing the love and memories that my mother left behind. I know that her passing was not the end, but a new beginning, a chance for me to grow and heal in ways I never thought possible. As I continue on this journey toward peace and acceptance, I hold onto the knowledge that my mother's love will always be with me, a guiding light in the darkness, a source of hope and healing in times of sorrow and despair.

High-Lights: Moving Forward with Love and Healing

AS I CONTINUE ON THIS journey toward peace and acceptance, I hold onto the knowledge that my mother's love will always be with me, a guiding light in the darkness, a source of hope and healing in times of sorrow and despair. And so I take each day as it comes, allowing myself to feel the pain and sorrow, but also embracing the love and memories that my mother left behind. I have learned to let go of the anger and bitterness that threatened

To consume me, and instead embrace the love and memories that my mother left with me. I have come to believe that my mother is not truly gone, but merely transformed, her spirit living on in the love and memories she left behind.

Grief is a journey, a path we must walk with courage and grace, allowing ourselves to feel the pain and sorrow without being consumed by it. But through the darkness, I found moments of light, small glimpses of hope and healing that helped me begin to find my way toward acceptance.

As I sit here, pen in hand, trying to find the words to express the depth of emotions swirling within me, I am reminded of the journey I have been on since the passing of my mother. In the months since my mother's passing, I have begun to find moments of peace and acceptance, small steps toward healing and hope. I have learned to forgive myself for the moments of anger, frustration, and sorrow that have consumed me in the wake of my mother's passing.

HEALING THROUGH GRIEF:
SURVIVING THE LOSS OF A LOVING PARENT

Most importantly, I thank God for being there in this time of pain and sorrow in my life. I know that her passing was not the end, but a new beginning, a chance for me to grow and heal in ways I never thought possible. I have learned to come to terms with my mother leaving me sooner than I planned, and I thank friends and family for being there to help guide me through this tumultuous time.

I also know that I am not alone, that my mother's love surrounds me, guiding me through the darkness toward the light. I have felt her presence in the gentle breeze that rustles the leaves, in the warmth of the sun on my face, and in the love and support of friends and family who have stood by my side through this grim time. Her presence was a source of comfort and strength, and her absence has left me feeling adrift, lost in a sea of sorrow and confusion, but I am strong, I'm a fight- er, that's who she taught me to be, and because of that, I will make it through this and become the person she's always wanted me to be.

In the aftermath of losing a parent, it can be incredibly difficult to imagine moving forward with love and healing. The pain of the loss will feel overwhelming, and it may seem impossible to find a way to navigate the grief that comes with such a profound loss. However, it is important to remember that healing is possible and that by approaching the grief process with love and compassion, it is possible to find a way to move forward in a healthy and positive way.

Ultimately, moving forward with love and healing after the loss of a parent is a deeply personal and individual process. There is no right or wrong way to grieve, and it is important to allow yourself the time and space you need to heal in your way. By approaching the grieving process with love and compassion, and by seeking out support from others who understand your pain, you can begin to find a path towards healing and begin to move forward in a positive and meaningful way

Bonuses Chapter 11: Still Fighting With Grief

The Last Fight For Complete Healing

What I didn't say in the Journal is what I'll share with you here in this Book. While my mother was fighting for her life, so was I at that time. I died twice in one night. I died in front o f my home, and I recall saying to one of the paramedics, I am dying aren't I, and my next recollection was darkness. The paramedics valiantly worked hard on me and brought me back. I remember seeing them working on me, it was around 2:00 a.m. when all of this took place.

At the time I did not realize I was having an outer body experience. The second time I die, I remember facing death head-on as I kept going in and out of consciousness. I remember feeling the cold grip of mortality tightening around me, etched into my memory with a surreal clarity. I remember the Second time I felt my spirit leave my body, floating above the chaos and confusion of the hospital room. I watched as doc- tors and nurses worked frantically to save me, their voices muffled and distant as I hovered on the edge of consciousness.

As I was in the hospital fighting for my life for several weeks, I had no clue that my mother was in the hospital fighting for her life at the same time. I found out she was fighting for her life on the day I was released from the hospital, as my family cared about me enough to not burden me with the fact that my mother and I were both in the hospital fighting for our lives.

She was so close that if I walked out of my room, turned right, walked six steps, and turned left, I would have seen her room.

The biggest regret that I still have, and that I fight with, is when I got out of the hospital, and went to her room to see her, she was asking me along with other people, is my son okay? I told my mother that I was out of the hospital, and I was okay because I didn't want her to be worried about me.

If I could go back in time and tell her that her son would be getting out of the hospital soon and he wanted to see her, I would have done so. I felt like she would have fought harder, but because I didn't say that it was like a piece came over her and she began to deteriorate. I blame myself and have been unable to stop blaming myself for that decision.

That decision to tell her the truth has become a burden that I carry with me every day. It colors my grief, taints my healing process, and leaves me wondering if I will ever find peace in the wake of such a profound loss. As I continue on my healing journey, I carry with me the lessons learned from the battles we fought together. I carry the knowledge that love transcends even the darkest of days, and that resilience can be found in the most unexpected of places. And I carry the understanding that grief, like love, is a profound and transformative force that shapes us in ways we never thought possible. And for that, I am grateful.

Through it all, I have learned to embrace the complexities of grief, to acknowledge the pain and the beauty that come hand in hand with loss. I have learned to find light in the darkness, to search for moments of joy and connection that can still be found even in despair. Most importantly, I have learned to cherish the memories of my mother, to hold onto them tightly as a beacon of hope and love in uncertainty.

Ruth Eleanor Beamon Tunstill
In loving Memorial
October 23, 1943 – May 10, 2023

Chapter 12: Understanding That It's Going To Take Time

Putting Up A Brave Front

It feels like a piece of my heart has been ripped out, leaving a void that can never truly be filled. Yet, despite the agonizing pain that accompanies such a loss, there is an expectation in society to put on a brave front, to soldier on as if everything is fine, to show the world that you are strong and capable of handling whatever life throws your way.

I can't stop thinking about watching her life passing away right in front of me, that memory causes a level of pain that hits me like a bomb going off inside of me, breaking me down into tears, as if the ground had been swept out from under me, leaving me struggling to find my footing in a world that had suddenly become unfamiliar and cold. In the days and weeks that followed her death, I found myself constantly trying to suppress my emotions, to hide my pain behind a stoic facade. I felt like I had to be the pillar of strength for my family.

But as the days turned into months, I realized that putting up a brave front was not sustainable. The grief I was trying so hard to bury deep within me was festering, growing stronger and more suffocating with each passing day. I knew that I needed to confront my pain head- on, to allow myself to feel the full magnitude of my loss, even if it meant showing vulnerability to the world.

HEALING THROUGH GRIEF:
SURVIVING THE LOSS OF A LOVING PARENT

It was a difficult journey, one filled with tears, anger, and moments of profound despair. But through it all, I am learning that true strength lies not in hiding your pain, but in facing it with courage and honesty.

I allowed myself to grieve openly, to cry until there were no more tears left to shed, to scream into the void and release the pent-up emotions that were threatening to consume me.

I also discovered the importance of self-care during this tumultuous time. I found solace in journaling, in talking to my sisters, and in sur- rounding myself with loved ones who understood the depth of my pain. I learned to forgive myself for the moments of weakness, for the days when getting out of bed felt like an insurmountable task.

Through this process, I'm realizing that healing is not linear journey. There are good days and bad days, moments of lightness and moments of darkness. There is no timeline for grief, no roadmap that tells you when you should be "over" your loss. Healing is a messy, chaotic process that unfolds at its own pace, and it is okay to take as much time as you need to come to terms with your new reality.

Remember that you are not alone in this journey. Reach out to others for support, seek out resources that can help you navigate the com- plex emotions that come with grief, and most importantly, be kind to yourself. You deserve love, compassion, and understanding, both from others and from yourself.

As I continue to navigate my own path of healing, I hold onto the memories of my mother, of the love and wisdom she imparted to me during her time on this earth. I carry her spirit with me, knowing that she will always be a part of me, guiding me through the darkest of days and lighting.

The Authors
BookBio

Angelo Quentin's book "Healing Through Grief: Surviving the Loss of a Loving Parent" offers a poignant and insightful exploration of the often difficult and complex journey of grieving the loss of a parent. Quentin brings a compassionate and practical approach to helping readers navigate the emotions and challenges that arise after the death of a parent.

The book is divided into several chapters, each on different aspects of the grieving process. In Chapter1, Quentin discusses the initial shock and overwhelming emotions that accompany the sudden loss of a parent. He emphasizes the importance of allowing oneself to feel and express these emotions in a healthy way, while also seeking support from loved ones and professionals.

In Chapter 2, Quentin delves into the concept of self-care and coping mechanisms for managing grief. He advises readers to prioritize their own well-being, both physically and emotionally, by engaging in activities that bring comfort and solace, such as exercise, meditation, or creative outlets.

Chapter 3 examines the unique dynamics of family relationships after the loss of a parent. Quentin provides guidance on how to navigate potential conflicts or misunderstandings that may arise within the family, and offers strategies for fostering open communication and unity during a time of grief.

One of the key themes throughout the book is the importance of honoring a parent's memory and finding ways to keep their spirit alive. In Chapter4, Quentin discusses various ways to pay tribute to a parent, whether through rituals, memorials, or storytelling. He emphasizes the healing power of remembering and celebrating the life of a loved one.

The book also addresses the challenges faced by grieving children and teens, offering valuable insights and resources for parents and caregivers in supporting young people through the grieving process. Quentin provides practical advice on helping children understand and cope with their emotions, and encourages open dialogue and reassurance.

Overall, "Healing Through Grief" is a valuable resource for anyone struggling with the loss of a parent. Quentin's compassionate and knowledgeable approach offers readers a roadmap for navigating their grief with grace and resilience. The book's practical strategies, insightful advice, and heartfelt anecdotes make it a comforting and empowering guide for those in need of support during a time of loss.

Call To Action

Attention:
I composed this Book and my Journal to assist those who had a loving parent to manage and heal from a very traumatizing life-altering event. This journal is based on self-healing, self-awareness of an emotional state of mind, and understanding we have the right to grieve, regardless of how long it takes to complete the process.

Interest:
My mom was a fantasy mother, she was strong, mindful, cherishing, supportive, caring, and loving, and because of that, I knew that I would never be alone. Regardless of how hard and intense life became throughout different periods of my life, she was always there to pick me up emotionally, mentally, and spiritually. I would like to share my journey with you of health healing.

Desired:
My Mother's Death: I was prepared for her death, and I realized it would come someday, when it finally happened, I became an emotional wreck for several months after her burial. It came to a point where I knew my mother would want me to move forward with my life to be happy, so I began the process of rebuilding myself and rebuilding my life utilizing strategies and techniques I would like to share with you in this book.

Action:
Together, let's take this journey of healing and learning how to deal with the pain so that we can have a productive life as our loving parents would have wanted for us.

Healing Through Grief: Surviving The
Loss Of A Loving Parent "The Book"
                    And
Healing Through Grief: Surviving The
Loss Of A Loving Parent "The Journal"